A

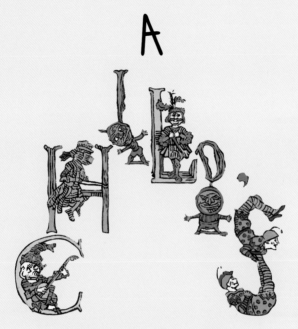

Machiavelli

A Child's Machiavelli

a primer
on power

Claudia Hart

PENGUIN
STUDIO

Penguin Studio
Published by the Penguin Group
Penguin Putnam Inc., 375 Hudson Street, New York, New York 10014, U.S.A.
Penguin Books Ltd, 27 Wrights Lane, London W8 5TZ, England
Penguin Books Australia Ltd, Ringwood, Victoria, Australia
Penguin Books Canada Ltd, 10 Alcorn Avenue, Toronto, Ontario, Canada M4V 3B2
Penguin Books (N.Z.) Ltd, 182-190 Wairau Road, Auckland 10, New Zealand
Penguin India, 210 Chiranjiv Tower, 43 Nehru Place, New Delhi, 11009 India

Penguin Books Ltd, Registered Offices: Harmondsworth, Middlesex, England

This edition published by Penguin Studio, 1998

10 9 8 7 6 5 4 3 2 1

Copyright © Claudia Hart, 1995, 1998. All rights reserved

This is an expanded edition of A Child's Machiavelli first published in 1995.

Cover from Rackham's Fairy Tale Coloring Book, ©1979 by Dover Publications, Inc.

Illustrations on pages 11, 24, and 25 are inspired by the work of Beatrix Potter. The
original Peter Rabbit Books⊖ are published by Frederick Warne & Co. Frederick Warne is
the owner of all rights, copyrights, and trademarks in the Beatrix Potter character names and
illustrations.

Grateful acknowledgment is made for permission to adapt and publish an illustration from
The Little Prince by Antoine de Saint-Exupery. ©1943, renewed 1971 and 1998 by
Harcourt Brace and Company. By permission of the publisher.

isbn 0-670-88021-3

cip data available

Designed by Joannah Ralston
Set in Memima
Printed in Singapore

Developed and
produced by:

VERVE
EDITIONS
Burlington,
Vermont

This book is dedicated to
Sylvia Bossu, 1962—1995.

Aside from thanking my mother,
Shirley Hart, and my husband, Alfonso
Rutigliano, who started the whole thing,
each in their own ways, I would like to thank
Christopher Sweet at Penguin Studio and Gary
Chassman at Verve Editions for believing
in my innate ability to be "both very smart
and very dumb at the same time."

Known as the father
of political science,
Niccolò Machiavelli lived
in Florence between
1469 and 1527.
<u>A Child's Machiavelli</u>
is based on <u>The Prince</u>,
his best-known work.

It's best to have a family
with a famous name 'cos then
you'll automatically impress
people and become really popular.

If you want to take over some place,
don't forget to kill not just the boss,
but also all his kids!

Either be really nice to people or kill 'em.
If you don't kill 'em and you're not so
nice, then they're gonna come after you.

If you just took over some place,
have a bunch of friends from your
old neighborhood go live there, too.
People won't even notice that these old
friends of yours are actually your spies.

If you just took over some place,
raise everybody's allowance.
Then people will think you really
like 'em, and you can do whatever
you want to 'em for a little while.

If you help make someone Big,
watch out. They're gonna wanna
get rid of you so everyone thinks
they did it alone.

Watch out for any new guy
in the neighborhood, 'specially when
he's popular. If you were bullying
all those wimps around before, then
maybe he's gonna get them all together
and they're all gonna gang up on you.

It's easy to take over some place with a really strong Chief. Everyone's used to being bossed around all the time, so when you get rid of him, people're barely gonna notice.

If you wanna take over a place run by
a guy with a bunch of his friends,
it's not so easy. If any of 'em help you,
they're probably gonna turn on you,
and the others you can't trust anyway.

If you wanna take over some place
where the people could decide for themselves,
you have to destroy **everything**,

'specially anyone who remembers, 'cos no one's
ever gonna listen to you as long as they can.

Never be afraid to beat
someone up if you have to.
First, try to talk 'em into
listening, but just in case,
you know what to do!

There are two kinds of people:
the Guys on the Top and the Guys
on the Bottom. The only thing the Big
Guys want is to get over on the
Little Guys and the only thing **they**
want is protection from the Big Guys.

The hardest job you can ever do is try to make things better for the Little Guys. The Big Guys are gonna hate your guts. And the Little Guys will be afraid to open their mouths.

Also, people never think that something new can be good. It's like trying to get your little brother to eat frog's legs...ugh!

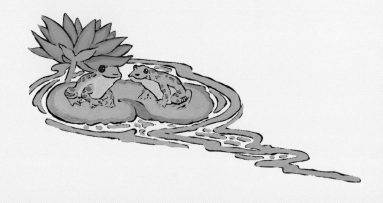

Sometimes the Guys on the Top
go too far. Then the Guys on the
Bottom get together to turn one
of their own people into a Boss.

When this happens, watch out!
It'll be really hard to get rid of him
'cos all the Little Guys are gonna
love him so much.

If a bunch of the Guys on the Top pull you up so now you're Boss, stay friends with your old pals on the Bottom. People always think Bosses are bad news, so when you surprise 'em with your niceness, they'll be so happy, they'll totally turn into your slaves!

Try to make everyone you know totally dependent on you, then you don't have to worry so much that they're gonna try to get rid of you.

When you take over some place,
kill off everyone who's
against you, pronto, then
act really nice to everyone left.

If people're scared of you at first,
you can boss 'em around easier later.
But if you're nice at first, they'll try
to get away with stuff and you're
gonna have to punish 'em all the
time. Then bad feelings about you
will stay in the air.

If you're already on the top, remember:
It's better to be popular with the Guys on
the Bottom than the Guys on the Top.

First, 'cos there's so much more of 'em.
Also, the Big Guys are so tricky that
you can **never** really trust 'em—
how do you think they got so Big?

Be nice to the people who are really dependent on you 'cos you don't have to worry about them turning on you.

But watch out for everyone else — 'cept for the chickenshits. If people go against you, the chickenshits will be too scared to join in anyway.

A gun is a man's best friend.

Only give things away
when people are watching.

If you wanna give presents to people,
make sure it's other people's stuff.

Even if people think you're cheap,
don't throw your money around.
'Cos if you lose your money and
start borrowing off them all the time,
then they're really gonna hate you.

If you're not a Boss but you
wanna be one, make sure
you trick everyone into thinking
you're a really generous guy.

Everyone says you should be nice
but no one really is, so if you do what
you should and be nice all the time,
you're probably gonna get screwed.

You can do **anything** to people.
As long as you don't steal
their girlfriends, they're never
really gonna hate you.

MOTHER

People who cheat
are always more successful
than people who
are honest.

When you cheat,
just don't let
anybody notice.

Make sure you only let people
see you doing stuff where you
come off looking really good.

Give the guys underneath you
all the dirty work to do.

Sometimes it's good to get people
pissed off at you just to show 'em
how little you care.

Never be wishy-washy.
You gotta say what you love
an' what you hate.

You're better off
having people scared of you
than liking you.

Now, it's okay if people are
scared of you. Just make sure
they don't hate you.

You gotta be tough.
People won't really like you then,
but they're probably only
your friends 'cos they think they
can get something off you.

Besides, most people
never really appreciate it
when you're being nice.

Every once in a while,
throw a big party and
invite all the Little People.

Be really nice
to your closest underlings.
Make them love you by
giving them lots of presents.

Don't give too many presents to people, 'cos you're gonna end up making yourself poor.

Then anyone who liked you
'cos of the presents is not
gonna like you anymore.

Support the arts and anything else
that improves the neighborhood.

It's best if the people in your gang
come from your same neighborhood.

Then you can make 'em feel good together by ganging up against everyone coming from somewhere else.

If somebody's got to hate you,
make sure it's a bunch of
weaklings with no money.

Don't keep your promises
if there's no reason to anymore —
nobody else does.

Don't worry if everyone says
you're no good,
as long as they know
who's boss!

Try not to hang around with people
stronger than you, 'cos if you
get stuck with 'em somewhere
an' they decide to turn on you,
then you're really in trouble.

Have five best friends
who you let tell what
they really think,
but only when you ask.

Stand up for your friends,
'cos if they get whipped,
they're gonna come after you.

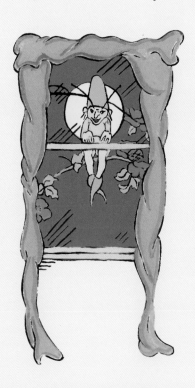

Claudia Hart is
an American artist who
for the last several years
has lived in Europe, moving
between Paris and Berlin.
She teaches, travels, and makes
exhibitions of her work
in Europe and in New York
City, where she now lives.
For information about the
work of Claudia Hart, please
contact Sandra Gering
Gallery, New York.
e-mail to: gering@interport.net